A Salute to the Charming City of Bremen

This city, which has grown and developed over 1200 years, can still today fascinate young and old alike. Once upon a time it was the donkey who urged the dog to "come with me to Bremen." And this is why you find the famous Town Musicians just round the corner behind the Town Hall. Touch one of the donkey's hooves and you'll be lucky your whole life long.

Bremen has many faces. One the one hand, it is an impressive, modern big city, with its docks, university, industry and innovative space technology. On the other hand, in the market place, in Böttcherstraße and the delightful little quarter known as the Schnoor, you can get a taste of the Golden Age of foreign trade and the Hanseatic League.

You can breathe deeply in Bremen. There is always a fresh breeze sweeping in off the North Sea and the many green areas of the city provide good, clean air. After seeing all the sights, there is a wonderful way of relaxing, by taking a boat out in the Bürgerpark (the Citizens' Park). Countless bicycle tracks invite you to explore the surrounding districts. And if you are fortunate enough to visit Bremen in May, don't miss a stroll through the Rhododendron Park. The blossom and the scent of azaleas and rhododendrons in all shades of red, yellow and white make it seem as if you are in fairy land.

The people of Bremen love celebrating. Whether it be the 600th birthday of Roland, a symbol of freedom for the city, or that of the Town Hall, a splendid Renaissance building, everyone joins in the fun. It might also be the annual carnival procession or the "Wallfest"; there is always something going on in Bremen.

Summer has scarcely said farewell when the city begins to look forward to its "fifth season". The "Freimarkt", an enormous fair, with breathtaking carousels and countless fairground booths, casts its spell over the city and its inhabitants.

And when the dull month of November sets in, it is a good time for walking along the Weser. With a mantle of fog lying on Café Sand and the ferry "Hal över", you can look forward to a nice, hot grog in the comfort of the Schnoor.

It is not only the eyes of the children that sparkle, when the lights of the Christmas fair are turned on. The Christmas fair in Bremen is the most beautiful and most romantic in the whole of North Germany.

These pictures are sure to make you want to see more of this wonderful city.

The historical market place invites you to linger, surrounded by magnificent medieval gabled houses.

The Town Hall has just celebrated its 600th birthday. A significant monument of the Weser Renaissance period, it epitomises the splendour of bourgeois affluence and is recognised as part of the world cultural heritage.

Roland has stood in front of the town hall since 1404. He symbolises the citizens' claims to the right to hold markets and to be free of the tutelage of the ruling archbishops. Roland too has become a part of the world cultural heritage.

In 1952, Gerhard Marcks created a bronze statue of the **Bremen Town Musicians.**

With its twin spires, the **Cathedral of St. Peter** stands as a defiant landmark on the highest point of the dune upon which Bremen's history once began.

The samba procession under the arcades of the Town Hall. Every February for many years, there has been a remarkable carnival celebration, featuring samba dancers in exotic costumes such as remind us of carnival in Rio.

The most impressive premises on the banks of the Weser are the historical **waterworks,** a listed building. Due to its characteristic shape it is also called the „umgedrehte Kommode", meaning the 'upside-down-commode'.

The "Bringer of Light" –
the Archangel Michael –
is a gold-plated bronze
relief by Hoetger, high
above the entrance to
the Paula Modersohn-
Becker Museum.

Böttcherstraße, situated
in the oldest part of
town between Schütting
and the Weser, is the ec-
centric creation of Lud-
wig Roselius, a mer-
chant of the town, who
had this street rebuilt
as a Gesamtkunstwerk
in the 1920s. Roselius
discovered decof-
feinated coffee and, in
1906, founded the
company HAG.

The "Roland von Bremen" is a perfect copy of the original Hanseatic "Kogge" (a medieval freighter, as it were), built in 1380. The ship has been converted into a museum and can be chartered for all sorts of celebrations.

Up to 1867, when the railway bridge was constructed, the **Schlachte** was Bremen's actual port. Today, it is the place where boat trips, both up- and downstream, begin.

In the Weserstadion football is king. And the local team, Werder Bremen, have often shown that they can play world-class football.

Pier 2 is also on the Weser. Where the old dockyards used to be, there is now a location for major live shows and concerts.

The Schnoor, the oldest part of Bremen, was originally the place where burghers and artisans lived. The houses in the narrow passageways, which have been restored with great care, remind us of pearls on a string (Schnur). Today, locals and tourists alike while away the hours in the arts and crafts shops and in the many cosy restaurants.

Up till 1950, flour was still ground in the **"Mühle am Wall".** Today you can sit in the midst of magnificent floral decoration and enjoy a meal or simply a cup of coffee.

The bronze sculpture of the pigs with their swineherd in the **Söge-straße,** which children are particularly fond of, is a reminder of the Low German name of the street: Söge = sows.

The Central Station is an impressive building, in neo-Renaissance style, designed in red and yellow brickwork by Herbert Stier.

The "Überseemuseum" (Overseas Museum) is right next to the station. Among the many attractions are African masks, Chinese popular art and "expeditions" to the South Seas.

The so-called **"old Bremer houses"** are proof that Bremen is a good place to live. First built in the 19th century, these house are still much favoured by the wealthier citizens.

The science centre known as **"Universum"** offers its visitors hands-on science. Inside this giant whale near the university, children as well as adults can experience how much fun a museum can be, when each visitor becomes a scientific researcher.

Approximately 150 metres high, the **"Fallturm"** is Bremen's highest building. In connection with space technology, it is used for conducting experiments in a state of weightlessness.

You only rarely see big "tubs" moored in the old **dockyards.** Since the arrival of containers and the demise of mixed cargoes, business here has gone downhill rapidly.

The Roland Mill in the docks is an old family firm, now in its 6th generation. It is the only mill of its kind in the whole of Germany.

In the Rhododendron Park, there are almost 3,000 sorts of rhododendron and azalea to be admired. Together with the botanical garden, the greenhouses and the "botanika", it is very popular with daytrippers.

The Bürgerpark and the adjoining Stadtwald (town woods) form a green oasis in the middle of the city. Children love to visit the animal compound, joggers and riders make use of tracks specially laid down for them and an additional pleasure is a trip in a boat around the "Emmasee".

Dammsiel – situated in the middle of Blockland – is a popular meeting-place for long- and short-distance cyclists. The Wümme is the perfect place to take a break and enjoy a picnic.

The jawbone of a whale displayed in Vegesack is a reminder that in former times, whale-hunters would set out from here on their dangerous voyages.

Castle Schönebeck – a baroque half-timbered building – was formerly a stately home. Now it is Vegesack's museum of local history, concentrating on shipping, ship-building, whale-hunting, fishing and sea rescue.

During **Freimarkt,** all of Bremen goes mad. What was formerly a trading fair with the travelling people has, since the 18th century, developed into a fantastic fun fair.

The ferry at **Sielwall, "Hal över",** carries passengers from the landing-stage at Ostertor-deich to the other side of the Weser. Awaiting you is a lovely sandy beach and a café.

The theatre "am Goethe Platz" belongs to the cultural centre of the city. Back in the Sixties, this theater was hotbed of avantgarde productions, creating the "Bremen style".

There is a spectacular view over the Weser from **Café Sand.** In the summer, you can play or lounge about on the beach and take a swim in the Weser.

Every year in December, the **Christmas Fair** in the oldest part of the city attracts countless visitors from all over Northern Germany. With its unique atmosphere, the sparkling lights and the myriad scents and perfumes in the air, it is a great way to get ready for the coming Christmas festival.

Photos: Klaus Stute

Text: Annette Zwilling

Translation: Geoff Hunter